The Vatican and the Holy See: The H
Catholic Church's G

By Charles Rive.

Adria Pingstone's picture of the Sistine Chapel

About Charles River Editors

Charles River Editors provides superior editing and original writing services across the digital publishing industry, with the expertise to create digital content for publishers across a vast range of subject matter. In addition to providing original digital content for third party publishers, we also republish civilization's greatest literary works, bringing them to new generations of readers via ebooks.

Sign up here to receive updates about free books as we publish them, and visit Our Kindle Author Page to browse today's free promotions and our most recently published Kindle titles.

Introduction

Michelangelo's painting of Daniel on the ceiling of the Sistine Chapel

The Vatican

Every year, millions visit a stunning circuit board city starring gorgeous collections of interconnected rectangular buildings and charming houses in shades of beige, sandy-brown, and other earthy tones. Zoom in a little closer, and one can see the Renaissance-style exterior of its buildings and the exquisite detail captured in the statues mounted on the tops of its palaces and cathedrals. Take a gander through the doors inside these historic places, and one enters a whole new world even more mesmerizing than the view of the city bathed in the peach and purple tints of sunset. Nested inside Rome, this spellbinding destination is none other than Vatican City.

The Vatican is an enchanting backdrop often found in literature, music, and the shimmering silver screen for good reason. Of course, being the smallest independent sovereignty in the world at just 44 hectares is a selling point that only scratches the surface. As the centuries-old home of the Catholic Church, its engrossing, eventful history, not to mention the rich and varied artwork and architecture contained within, ensures the influence and importance of the Vatican far surpasses its size.

While the Vatican is best known for being the ultimate center of Roman Catholicism today, one might be surprised to learn that once upon a time, this area was a haven for pagan worship. Before the 1st century CE, the *Ager Vaticanus*, the forerunning name of the city, referred to the territories to the west of the Tiber River. This territory stretched from the Janiculum Hill to the

Monte Mario, with the *Mons Vaticanus*, or Vatican Hill, sitting in its center. For the most part, the marshy lands of the *Ager Vaticanus* were inhabitable; whatever land the farmers managed to tame produced little to no crops, and according to Cicero, the famous Roman politician who lived in the 1st century BCE, the grapes were sour and the wine made from it rancid. The only sign of life seemed to have been found in a now extinct Etruscan town named "*Vaticum*" on Vatican Hill. This may have been the etymological source of "*Vaticanus*," and later, its shortened form, "Vatican."

The Vatican and the Holy See: The History and Legacy of the Roman Catholic Church's Governing Body examines the remarkable impact the Vatican has had on the world over nearly 2,000 years. Along with pictures of important people, places, and events, you will learn about the Vatican like never before.

The Vatican and the Holy See: The History and Legacy of the Roman Catholic Church's Governing Body

About Charles River Editors

Introduction

   Pagan Origins and Early Christianity

   The Death of Paganism, Constantine, and the Papal States

   Schisms, Reconciliation, and Resurgence

   Too Many Cooks in the Kitchen

   Clash of the Republics, the Risorgimento, and the Modern Day Vatican

   Online Resources

   Bibliography

Free Books by Charles River Editors

Discounted Books by Charles River Editors

Pagan Origins and Early Christianity

"And this gospel of the kingdom will be preached in all the world as a witness to all the nations, and then the end will come." – Matthew 24:14

Following the rise of the Roman Empire in the later 1st century BCE, Vatican Hill began to attract more people. Agrippina the Elder, the mother of the notorious Emperor Caligula, extracted all the excess water from the lands, rolled out her first batch of gardens, and had workers tend to the area to prep it for new construction projects. Subsequently, the suburban town evolved to a bustling complex dotted with handsome villas and seasonal homes owned by emperors and those in the upper echelons of society. Alongside these spacious estates were mausoleums and pagan churches dedicated to an assortment of Roman gods and other polytheistic religions.

Luis Garcia's picture of a bust of Agrippina the Elder

Ironically, some historians believe the area's role as a pagan sacred space was how the word "Vatican" actually came about. The local oracles and traveling seers who frequented the area were nicknamed the "*Vaticania*," a derivative of the Latin word *"vates,"* meaning "tellers of the future." The hill soon became typecasted as a place where squadrons of fortunetellers set up shop, accosting passersby with reading offers, and pushing their fortunetelling knickknacks.

Also on the hill was a standing stone erected to symbolize the area's sanctity, and a temple built in honor of Cybele, the serpent goddess of the earth, called the *"Phrygianum."* In Anatolian mythology, Cybele, a ravishing deity with flowing caramel locks in her human form, wore a mural crown. This was a grand headpiece that resembled the city's defensive walls. Her disciples called her the "Mountain Mother," and often presented sacrifices of special crops to her on the crest of the hill in return for the safety of their families and the general well-being of Rome. Her followers hoped to be enlightened by the goddess' secrets of life, death, and reincarnation.

Interestingly enough, as blasphemous as it might sound to Christians, the religions bear striking similarities, which have led some chroniclers to conclude that many elements of Christianity were lifted from the pagan religion. For one thing, Cybele's son, Attis, was supposedly born on the 25th of December and was also a "crucified god." Cybele's followers celebrated the death and resurrection of Attis as Christians do with Christ with a 3-day festival in late March. Attis's "Bloody Day," celebrated on the 24th of March, has since been turned to "Good Friday," and his "Day of Joy" on the 26th is now "Easter Sunday." Furthermore, the term "Easter" itself was taken from Cybele's sister, Ishtar, a fertility goddess.

In the year 40 CE, the young, tortured, and possibly deranged Emperor Caligula cleared a section of one of his mother's gardens, and commissioned the construction of a horse-racing establishment there. This chariot stadium was called the "Circus of Gaius," and later, the "Circus of Nero," when the circus changed hands. Unlike the traditional round Colosseum of Rome, circuses were oblong or rectangular in shape, and its racing tracks were located on the ground floor. The establishment initially hosted private horse races for the emperor and selected guests, but was later made open to the public for the occasional holiday or festival.

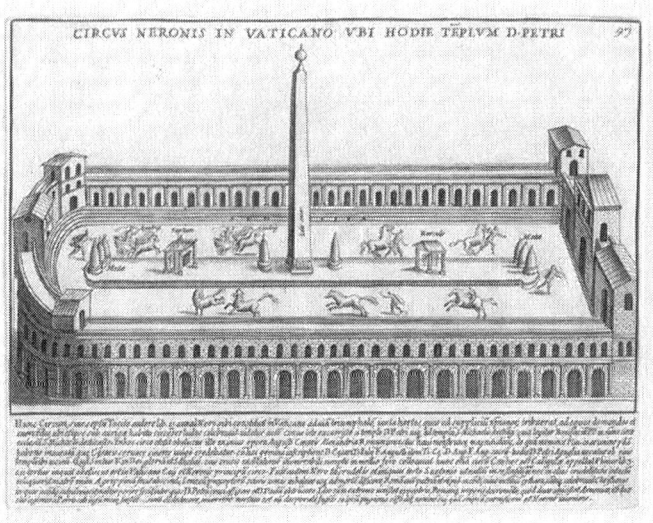

A 17th century sketch of the Circus of Nero

A *spina,* which was a divider adorned with intricately carved columns and pillars, split the track in two but was cut short on either end to create a semi-oval track. 3 years earlier, Caligula had personally brought home an elegant "rose-colored obelisk" from his trip in Egypt, and he positioned it in the heart of the *spina.* The obelisk was already considered an antique at the time, for it had been built in 1835 BCE by Pharaoh Mencares as a tribute to the sun. To those in Heliopolis, where the obelisk was birthed, the "city of the sun" sat in the center of the universe, and the obelisk was considered a symbol of "the sacred flow of life between heaven and earth." The spectators were seated in seats on different levels facing the track.

Louis le Grand's picture of a bust of Caligula

Around this time, the seeds of a new religion that had been planted by the roaming apostle, Paul, began to stir. Paul, formerly a Jewish man named Saul, was not a participant of Christ's arrest or death, but he had played an active role in wiping out several Christian churches in Jerusalem. And while he might have been guilt-free when it came to Christ's death, Paul was said to have contributed to the execution of St. Stephen, the world's first Christian martyr.

Paul's bloodlust for Christians would have continued unchecked if it were not for one fateful campaign to annihilate more Christians in Damascus. There, he was washed over by the light of the Lord, and following a deep period of repentance, he converted to Christianity. He then partnered up with Barnabas, an ex-Jew from Cyprus, and vowed to spread the gospel wherever the Holy Spirit guided them.

The pair proceeded to embark on 3 missionary expeditions. The duo started small, and while they left the church at Syria, opted to stick around and preach at local synagogues. When they realized their brand of Christianity was a dud among the neighborhood Jews, the pair decided to turn their attention to converting the Gentiles (non-Jews). They left Syria and traveled to Cyprus, then onward to the territories of Asia Minor, including the region of present-day Turkey. It was there that karma snuck up on him, for the one-time heckler had become the heckled. His words often riled up the potential converts – so much so that he was pummeled and thrown behind bars on a regular basis. On one occasion, he was cornered by an unruly mob, stoned, and left for dead.

Nevertheless, Paul's spirit refused to waver, and he forged forward with his journey. His second expedition took him back to Antioch, where he set up a church, then to Cyprus once more. From there, he steered his ship towards the west of Asia Minor, and later, to a cluster of small islands on the coast of Greece. Here, Paul found luck with the much more malleable minds of the Athenians on Mars Hill. He managed to garner a small following, but when he was invited to explain the concept of a non-materialistic god to Athenian philosophers, he was laughed off the stage.

For Paul's third and final expedition, he returned to Asia Minor and escalated his campaigns there. He reprogrammed the believers of the occult and established a string of churches around the region. When his work was finished there, he headed for Rome.

Christian conversion in Rome was a rarity, especially because doing so was practically the equivalent of signing one's own death warrant. Christianity was made illegal by the Roman emperors, as the people were expected to bow before the emperor, and the emperor alone. Many of these converts were slaves and peasants promised a better life by the evangelists. On top of having to scrape by each day, their lives were made more miserable by the risk of getting caught, for being outed as a Christian back then simply meant death. Paul himself was beheaded when nabbed by Roman authorities. Legend has it that many of Rome's first Christians were tossed into lion dens, or made to face off with and inevitably wolfed down by a beast of a similar size in the Colosseum.

Thanks to Emperor Nero, the unpopularity of Christianity among the Roman people only worsened. In mid-July of 64 CE, a terrible fire erupted in the shopping center close to the Circus Maximus, one of Rome's largest chariot stadiums. Despite the firefighters' best efforts, the flames raged on for 6 days, eventually spreading to the slums. The dry, wooden buildings and harsh gusts of winds acted as its accelerant, and by the time the flames were contained, nearly 67% of the city was nothing but rubble and debris, large chunks of which hid dozens of corpses. Among the casualties of the fire were the Temple of Jupiter Stator, the Atrium Vestae, and hundreds of Romans, while thousands wept over the scorched remnants of their homes.

A bust of Nero

What appears most likely is that the fire was an accident, likely caused by flammable materials near the Circus Maximus. Indeed, blazes of such kind were common until the 19th century, in overcrowded cities with wooden houses closely packed together, lit and heated by open flames and with no organized official fire brigades. Rome would suffer two more major fires in the next 15 years.

However, the grapevines were soon abuzz with rumors that Emperor Nero was the culprit. Many speculated that it was his desperate attempt at snaking around the stifling senate so that he could renovate Rome as he so pleased. Though there was plenty of evidence to suggest that Nero was more than 35 miles away when the fire began, he opted for the easy way out by pointing his finger at the Christians. The secretive sect, which still boasted only small numbers but was fast growing in popularity, was viewed with suspicion and even hatred, as the Jews also were, by much of the Roman Empire. The main reason for this dislike was simple: the other pagan polytheistic traditions which flourished side by side throughout the empire might advocate the superiority of their own particular gods but, unlike the Christians, would not deny the existence of others. Christians flat-out believed that theirs was the only true God, and were not afraid to say so. Consequently, they were highly unpopular.

Nero capitalised on that unpopularity by accusing Christians of being responsible for the blaze, though it does not appear as though any motive was ever ascribed to them. Several were seized and, after being tortured, confessed (it is unclear whether they confessed to being Christians, or to the arson itself, but most sources are in accord in saying that they confessed *because* they were tortured). Scores of Christians were martyred, some draped in the skins of wild animals and then torn apart by dogs in the arena, others crucified in a mockery of Jesus's martyrdom, and still more were burned alive, nightly, to serve as illumination for Nero's garden banquets. The first institutionalised persecution of the Christians in the history of the Roman Empire (but not the last) had begun.

Tacitus described Nero's scapegoating of the Christians, writing, "Consequently, to get rid of the report, Nero fastened the guilt and inflicted the most exquisite tortures on a class hated for their abominations, called Christians by the populace. Christus, from whom the name had its origin, suffered the extreme penalty during the reign of Tiberius at the hands of one of our procurators, Pontius Pilatus, and a most mischievous superstition, thus checked for the moment, again broke out not only in Judaea, the first source of the evil, but even in Rome, where all things hideous and shameful from every part of the world find their centre and become popular. Accordingly, an arrest was first made of all who pleaded guilty; then, upon their information, an immense multitude was convicted, not so much of the crime of firing the city, as of hatred against mankind. Mockery of all sorts was added to their deaths. Covered with the skins of beasts, they were torn by dogs and perished, or were nailed to crosses, or were doomed to the flames and burnt, to serve as a nightly illumination, when daylight had expired."

Nero, along with the line of Christianity-detesting successors that followed, worked day in and day out to keep the dangerous religion from taking flight in Rome. Like the flames that ran wild in July of 64, however, the religion would spread, which would have had Nero and his successors spinning in their graves. Christianity was more than just here to stay – Rome was about 250 years away from becoming the crowning center and beating heart of Western Christianity.

The Death of Paganism, Constantine, and the Papal States

"By keeping the Divine faith, I am made a partaker of the light of truth...Hence...I profess the most holy religion...I have aroused each nation of the world in succession to a well-grounded hope for security...so that those which, groaning...to the most cruel tyrants...and daily sufferings, had...been utterly destroyed, [and] have been restored through my agency to a far happier state."
– Letter of Constantine to the Persian King Sapor

One might think that the threat of death looming over their heads would be incentive enough for Roman Christians to break away from the faith, but in the face of the persecutions, a fraction of these Roman Christians persevered.

First of all, what was it about the Christians that made them targets of such fear and hatred, anyway? Most Romans, who were "conservatives" that adhered strictly to Roman polytheistic beliefs, found the Christian belief of a single deity that granted salvation both preposterous and a hazard to their system. The pagan Romans believed that the Christians' refusal to participate with local customs defiled the purity of the *pax deorum*, which was essentially the people's spiritual treaty with the gods. Only under the *pax deorum*, which required sacrifices and dutiful worship from its people, would the gods grant peace and protection to the cities and towns of the empire.

Those who refused to kowtow or present gifts to the emperor were also pegged as national traitors. The Christians rejected this tradition, claiming that the emperor was only human and therefore not worthy of such veneration. Authorities suspected that Christian Masses, which excluded non-Christians, were merely disguises for gatherings where conspirators plotted to overthrow the government.

The false rumors surrounding the Christians did even less to help their plight. Many Romans misunderstood the sacrament of the Eucharist, and thought Christianity to be a growing cult that revolved around cannibalism. Others misinterpreted the Christian idea of agape, defined as "selfless, sacrificial, and unconditional love," and the most sacred of the 4 types of love in the Bible. Stories about these Christian "love feasts" also leaked to the authorities. While these were none more than innocent festivals that celebrated platonic love of the "brothers and sisters" of the Church, Romans took them as debauched orgy-filled carousals that glorified incest and promiscuity.

Like many societies of early civilization, authorities branded the Christians, whom they regarded as criminals, with tattoos. Some Christian captives, slaves included, were forcibly inked with crosses and other Christian symbols on their foreheads, making it impossible for them to deny their faiths. Those sporting the faded ink were almost always sentenced to a lifetime in the mines and other areas of backbreaking manual labor.

It was for these very reasons that the surviving Christians had no choice but to duck out of sight and resume their operations underground, worshiping and holding meetings in the homes of wealthy members and the basements of strange mausoleums. But rather than fizzle out like Mithraism, Manichaeism, and other early pagan factions and cults eventually did, there were a number of factors that cemented Christianity's place in Rome. Apart from those who were won over by the religion's message of forgiveness, salvation, and an eternal life of peace, the chaotic state of 3rd century Rome attracted as many souls as it turned away. The devils of violent incursions and the plague had the terrified souls who were seeking for a way out find an exit – or in this case, an entrance – in Christianity. Others were moved by the many Christians who volunteered to cater to the sick during plague seasons, a job that most other Romans avoided at all costs. Many of those who survived the disease and other hardships under Christian wings would also later join the movement "out of loyalty."

A great portion of these Christian converts were women, for the early version of the religion advertised a platform of equality for all people, notwithstanding gender, status, or background. One pro-pagan writer, Celsus, called it a "religion for women, children, and slaves." It was precisely these characteristics that the pro-pagan writer, Celsus, found fault with, but they made the budding religion even more appealing to a larger number of people. For what would prove to be a limited time only, women were allowed to serve as deaconesses. Other Christian women who acted as housewives may have also contributed to the breeding of a new Christian generation.

Moreover, the stories of martyrdom, which contained both underdogs and gore, were an instant hit with the masses. Yet another crucial factor that led to the rapid spread of the religion was the display of cool and unyielding bravery the most famous of the Christian martyrs exhibited when confronted with certain death. There was the story of Polycarp, who was arrested when he refused to burn incense for the emperor. In the spirit of tit-for-tat, the young man, a disciple of the apostle John, was sent to the stakes, but when the flames licking him would not kill him, he was put out of his misery via a stab to the chest.

Naturally, women martyrs struck a chord with female audiences. There was St. Agnes, a gorgeous virgin who angered her suitors by claiming Christ as her spouse. When her admirers-turned-stalkers could not face the humiliation of their rejected advances, they turned her in to authorities. Agnes was then seized by the local police, stripped of her clothes, tethered to a team of temperamental horses, and dragged through the streets, stark naked. Almost at once, thick, coarse hairs miraculously sprouted from every pore on her body to cushion her from the ragged surface of the streets. Anyone who even so much as glanced at her the wrong way was "struck blind" on the spot. Agnes was finally hoisted back to her feet, shaken, but otherwise unscathed, then transported to the stakes. When the kindling under the seemingly indestructible Agnes would not burn, a soldier at his wit's end took matters into his own hands and finished off the job with a swift swing of his sword.

Though Christianity was steadily picking up steam in Rome, it would not have been so established if it were not for the imperial endorsement it eventually won. Emperor Constantine I, otherwise known as Constantine the Great, was born to a well-respected officer in the Roman army, and a peasant-born mother, who might have either been the wife or concubine of his father, in Moesia (now Siberia). Whatever the case, in 289, his father divorced his birth mother, scooped up his 9-year-old son, packed up their belongings, and left for Rome. There, his father married the daughter of Western Roman Emperor Maximian, and was promoted to "deputy emperor," or the second-in-command to the imperial crown.

The head of Constantine from a statue, now housed at the Metropolitan Museum of Art in New York City

Meanwhile, Constantine was sent off to live in the court of Emperor Diocletian in the eastern neck of the empire. Here, he received a formal education under the best scholars the Eastern Empire had to offer. He was trained in Latin and Greek, and studied a blend of both pagan and Christian theology, which some say helped to broaden his horizons at an early age.

On the year of his 23rd birthday, Diocletian spearheaded a fresh empire-wide campaign against the Roman Christians, which has since been memorialized as the "10th Persecution." The emperor was aggravated by the growing population of Christians in his empire, and his abhorrence of the Christians only exacerbated by the simultaneously growing wealth of their communities. Starting in February of 303, imperial soldiers descended upon Nicomedia, where they burst through the doors of Christian churches, looted all their sacred texts and objects, and hurled them into bonfires. The captured churches were then torched and burned to the ground.

What came after was a merciless imperial decree that ordered the demolition of the remaining Christian properties in or around the neighborhood. From Nicomedia, they worked their way to Marseilles, Sicily, Milan, and more. The entire city of Phrygia, where the Christians vastly outnumbered the pagans, vanished in the flames, along with every last one of its residents. For the next decade, Christians were shackled and imprisoned in droves. Galerius, the adopted son of Diocletian, hired a band of experienced arsonists to set the imperial palace alight. He hoped to pin the blame on the Christians, and turn up the heat on the Christian persecution. As a result, thousands of Christians, men and women, young and old, lost their lives in the bloody frenzy. Some, trapped in their blazing homes, were burned alive, or suffocated from smoke inhalation. Some succumbed to fatal wounds they received from week-long interrogation and torture sessions, which often featured scourges and blades. Others had their hands cuffed behind their backs, and chains weighed down with stones wrapped around their necks and bodies. Their chains were then latched onto the chains of the prisoner next to them, and shoved into the sea, where they sunk down to the black abyss.

Imperial princes and governors who became bored of the repetitive slaughtering were given free rein to explore their gruesome imaginations. These sadistic individuals were said to have targeted those excused from execution. Unwilling to allow the Christians to get off scot-free, these officials chose to mutilate the newly-exonerated by snipping off their noses and ears, snapping their limbs into pieces, and other Joker-inspired makeovers. The horror stories went on and on. Constantine later claimed to have voiced his opposition to the brutal treatment of Christians during this time, but historians today believe otherwise.

In 305, Constantine's father replaced Maximian at the throne as Emperor Constantius I. Constantine, a natural on the battlefield, joined his father in Britain, and was thrust into the public eye when the Roman forces triumphed and Constantius was declared "Britannicus Maximus II." By the next year, however, Constantius had fallen ill, and on his deathbed, he recommended his son as his successor. When his illness took him in July, Constantine was handed the crown, and was thereby known as Emperor Constantine I.

At this point, a chain of civil wars had broken loose in the Roman Empire, further ripping apart the already delicate tetrarchy (any system operating under 4 different powers) established by Diocletian. Constantine squared off with Maxentius for control of the western empire, the son of Maximian, while Diocletian squabbled with Licinius, the other ruler of the eastern empire. In 312, Constantine led his humble army to Italy, where they were scheduled to battle with Maximian's much larger and more seasoned troops at the Milvian Bridge by the Tiber River.

According to both Eusebius and Lactantius, two of the emperor's principal biographers, the day before the battle Constantine was stricken by a vision. Lactantius claims that Constantine was visited by an angel as he dreamt the night before battle, while Eusebius's version is even more theatrical. According to Eusebius, while Constantine's army was on the march, a fiery symbol, shaped like the crossed X and P of the Latin Alphabet (☧) and bearing beneath it the legend "*Ἐν Τούτῳ Νίκα*" ("by this sign, you will conquer"), appeared in the sky above. The X and P represented the Greek letters Xhi and Rho, the first two letters of Christ's name in the

Greek spelling.

Constantine might have brushed it off as a psychedelic-induced vision if it were not for the dream he had that night. He was said to have been visited by Christ himself during his slumber, who instructed him to paint the *labarum* (an "X" superimposed on a "P," ancient Greek letters that spelled "Christ") onto the shields of his soldiers. First thing the next morning, he did just that, and later crowned the *labarum* on his own shield with "a wreath of gold and precious stones." Later that day, Constantine's forces defeated Maxentius' forces with effortless ease. It was this victory that fortified the foundations of Constantine's Christian beliefs, making him the first Christian emperor of the Roman Empire.

Presumably, such a divine manifestation would have prompted an almost immediate conversion, and Constantine certainly alluded to that in later propaganda, but there is significant evidence that the original manifestation was actually viewed as a pagan divine revelation. In that version, the revelation was interpreted as being the halo of *Sol Invictus,* the Sun God with whom Constantine claimed a long-standing association and whose iconography was depicted in coins issued by Constantine even years after the battle.

This gold coin, minted in 313, depicts Constantine with *Sol Invictus*

One problem with the theory that Constantine merely observed what he thought was a divine revelation from *Sol Invictus* is that accounts agree he changed the appearance of his equipment before the battle. Some scholars have rather optimistically suggested that the fiery symbol was in fact a sun dog, but whatever the source of Constantine's divine inspiration, whether miraculous, scientific or simply clever propaganda, on the day of battle his armies apparently approached Maxentius's forces with the Xhi Rho painted on their shields. According to Eusebius, "Assuming therefore the Supreme God as his patron, and invoking His Christ to be his preserver and aid, and setting the victorious trophy, the salutary symbol, in front of his soldiers and body-guard, he marched with his whole forces, trying to obtain again for the Romans the freedom they had inherited from their ancestors."

Given the result of the impending battle, Eusebius attributed Maxentius's decision-making during the fighting to divine intervention as well, writing:

"And already he was approaching very near-Rome itself, when, to save him from the necessity of fighting with all the Romans for the tyrant's sake, God himself drew the tyrant, as it were by secret cords, a long way outside the gates. And now those miracles recorded in Holy Writ, which God of old wrought against the ungodly (discredited by most as fables, yet believed by the faithful), did he in every deed confirm to all alike, believers and unbelievers, who were eye-witnesses of the wonders. For as once in the days of Moses and the Hebrew nation, who were worshipers of God, "Pharaoh's chariots and his host hath he cast into the sea and his chosen chariot-captains are drowned in the Red Sea," --so at this time Maxentius, and the soldiers and guards with him, 'went down into the depths like stone,' when, in his flight before the divinely-aided forces of Constantine, he essayed to cross the river which lay in his way, over which, making a strong bridge of boats, he had framed an engine of destruction, really against himself, but in the hope of ca-snaring thereby him who was beloved by God. For his God stood by the one to protect him, while the other, godless, proved to be the miserable contriver of these secret devices to his own ruin. So that one might well say, 'He hath made a pit, and digged it, and is fallen into the ditch which he made. His mischief shall return upon his own head, and his violence shall. come down upon his own pate.'

Thus, in the present instance, under divine direction, the machine erected on the bridge, with the ambuscade concealed therein, giving way unexpectedly before the appointed time, the bridge began to sink, and the boats with the men in them went bodily to the bottom. And first the wretch himself, then his armed attendants and guards, even as the sacred oracles had before described, 'sank as lead in the mighty waters.' So that they who thus obtained victory from God might well, if not in the same words, yet in fact in the same spirit as the people of his great servant Moses, sing and speak as they did concerning the impious tyrant of old: 'Let us sing unto the Lord, for he hath been glorified exceedingly: the horse and his rider hath he thrown into the sea. He is become my helper and my shield unto salvation.' And again, 'Who is like unto thee, O Lord, among the gods? who is like thee, glorious in holiness, marvelous in praises, doing wonders?'

Regardless, the next year, Constantine arranged for a meeting with Licinius in Milan, where they proceeded to draw up and formalize the Edict of Milan. This decree not only halted the persecution of Christians, it rendered the religion legitimate in the eyes of the law. Other than the banning of gladiator shows, Constantine also ensured that any Jews who stoned other Jews for hopping on the Christian bandwagon would be severely punished. As the icing on top of the cake, all surviving properties seized by previous emperors and officials were duly returned to their rightful owners. Furthermore, Christians, along with citizens that belonged to any other religious group, were granted the freedom to build their own places of worship, and practice their faiths freely in public.

When Licinius, by now the only Emperor of the Eastern Empire, attempted to repeal the edict 3 years later, relations between the two emperors deteriorated. In 324, Constantine's forces squashed Licinius's men and knocked him out of the picture completely. Constantine unified the east and west, and as sole sovereign of the Roman Empire, he legalized Christianity in all of his territories, new and old. The emperor then proceeded to construct his new capital in the east, specifically Byzantium (now Istanbul), which he christened "Constantinople." Byzantium was rebranded "*Nova Roma*," or "New Rome." There, he built a slew of churches devoted to the Christian God, as well as a Senate and civic offices modeled after old Rome.

Around 326, Constantine orchestrated and assembled a team for the construction of what is now called the "Old St. Peter's Basilica," a sacred establishment that took 3 decades to build but would stand for the next 1,200 years. The new establishment was to be built on the old Vatican Hill, and its main chapel constructed directly on top of the site of Emperor Nero's now dismantled circus. The rest of the basilica, now considered the "Mother Church of Roman Catholicism," rested on the burial ground of Nero's countless victims.

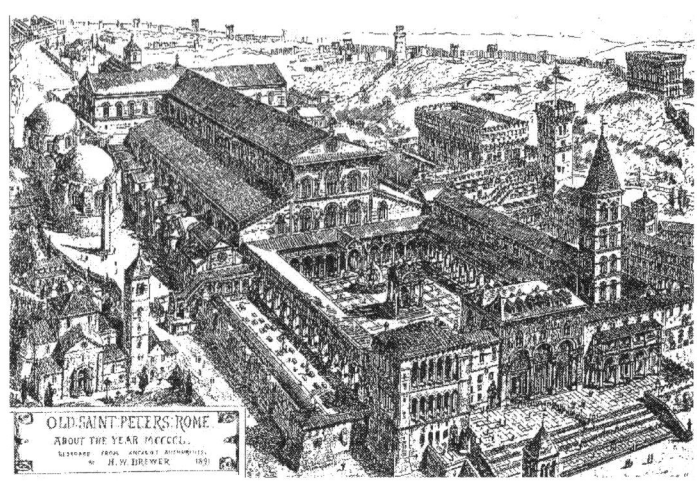

A depiction of Old St. Peter's Basilica and its surroundings in the 15th century, including the obelisk Caligula had placed there in the 1st century CE

Upon its completion, the rectangular complex featured a "5-aisled basilica" with connecting brown buildings, a tower with a domed roof, and a courtyard paved in stone in its center. The unroofed entrance hall of the church was named "Paradise," which contained a pretty garden with trickling fountains. The nave, or body of the church, bore an arch with mosaic portraits of St. Peter (the alleged first pope of Rome) and Constantine, fashioned out of colored glass. All 4 walls of the chapel were decorated with frescoes of biblical scenes and more portraits of Christian patriarchs. 2 years later, Pope Sylvester I blessed the basilica and named it the center for Christian pilgrimages.

Though it is now a common held belief that it was Constantine who made Christianity the official religion of the empire, this fact has since been debunked. Rather, it was Emperor Theodosius who sealed the deal in 380, with an act that marked the transition of early Pauline Christianity to the Roman Catholic Church. Between 389 and 391, Theodosius published the self-tited "Theodosian decrees," which banned paganism, sanctioned the persecution of pagans, and made the worship of other gods illegal. Constantine was reportedly no more than a pioneer who loosened the lock, but it was Theodosius who kicked that door wide open.

As a matter of fact, Constantine is believed to have remained somewhat impartial to both Christianity and pagan religions, even towards the latter half of his life. For instance, though the cross was a symbol minted on one of his coins, other currency during his reign featured Mars, the Roman god of war, and Sol Invictus, the sun god. Moreover, he never retired his title of "*pontifex maximus*," the "chief priest of the state cult." Even more curiously, some chroniclers doubt the authenticity of Constantine's conversion altogether, going so far as to suggest that his motivations behind doing so were purely political.

Somewhat fittingly, the dawn of the papacy is another muddled subject. According to Catholic archives, it was Christ who handpicked one of his favorite apostles, St. Peter, to be his "earthly representative." This is a theory backed by the biblical passage found in Chapter 16 of Matthew, which reads, "Thou art Peter, and upon this rock, I will build my church. I will give thee the keys to the kingdom of heaven." These same words are now found engraved around the dome of St. Peter's Basilica. These representatives, known as "popes" – or the bishops of Rome – that succeeded the apostle are described as the "symbolic descendants" of Peter, with an exclusive seat at "Peter's Chair," his coveted throne.

Other historians have since dismissed the idea of Peter as the first pope, suggesting that the real identity of the earliest bishop may never be resolved. The only tangible proof involving the early years of the papacy can be found in records that highlight the existence of a "committee of elders," instead of a singular ruling body, known as the *"presbyteroi."* It was only in the 2nd century that letters from Ignatius of Antioch shed light on Christian churches, and that they were led by one bishop alone.

The *Domus Laterani*, or the Lateran Palace, landed in the hands of Constantine when he wedded his second wife and the sister of Maxentius, Fausta. Formerly known as the *"Domus Faustae,"* or the "House of Fausta," the princely palace was situated in the Piazza San Giovanni of southeast Rome. Following the issuing of the Edict of Milan in 313, the property was leased to Pope Melchiades. Melchiades then marshaled the first assemblage of bishops of the Church, and moved into the palace. The Lateran would serve as the official home and headquarters of the papacy for the next millennium, and it would eventually become the "Vatican of the Middle Ages."

A medieval depiction of the Lateran Palace

Papal dominion over central Italy was a movement that was sparked as early as the mid-5th century, when Pope Leo was seated at Peter's Chair. In 451, the year Attila the Hun declared his intentions to seize Rome, Leo was among the team of head negotiators who managed to persuade the potential invaders from sacking the city.

Raphael's painting depicting Leo meeting Attila

By the time Pope Gregory I rose to power in 590, the Roman emperor was nothing but a puppet controlled by the Catholic Church. The people shuffled forward and nestled up even closer against the papal bosom under Gregory's reign, for the pope had aided with the refugee situation when they faced invasion from the Lombards, and had even helped to cool things down, creating a temporary bout of peace that lasted for some time.

By this time, Sardinia, Sicily, and some cities neighboring Rome were placed under papal control, and were collectively known as the "Patrimony of St. Peter." While these lands technically fell under the ownership of the empire, papal officials had the last say at the end of the day. As the papacy continued to thrive in the public eye, it dawned on the Roman Catholic Church that it was time to shrug off the extra baggage and take the reins for themselves.

Emperor Justinian was the last Roman-born monarch of the Eastern Roman Empire. His death in 565 cued the rise of the Greek-speaking and chiefly Christian Byzantine Empire. The Byzantine emperors would possess far greater powers than their Western counterparts, for they believed in the divine right of kings, which dictated that their right to rule had been granted to them by God Himself. With the Church and the rest of the officials crammed in the backseat as the emperor rode solo up front, it did not take long for those in the rear to lose their heads. Starting from the early years of the 8th century, Pope Gregory II, and his successor, Gregory III, began to distance themselves from the Byzantine Empire. The Church was disgruntled enough by the tax spike and Constantinople's inability to keep Rome out of harm's way. What really grinded their gears was the Iconoclastic Controversy of 730, when Emperor Leo III formally banned the worship of icons and religious images.

When the Lombard invaders captured Ravenna in the 750s, Pope Stephen II spotted an opportunity. The pope organized a meeting with Frankish King Pepin the Short and presented him with a proposition. In exchange for a few Italian territories, Pepin would receive the papal assistance he hopelessly needed. In 756, Pepin succeeded in driving Aistulf, the Lombard leader, and his forces out of Italy. Keeping his word and ignoring Emperor Leo's outstretched hands, the king gifted Stephen the Italian cities of Ravenna and a confederacy of 5 cities known as the "Pentapolis": Ancona, Pesaro, Rimini, Senigallia, and Fano. Apart from the papal support, this was Pepin's token of gratitude to the Church for recognizing him as the rightful King of the Franks. This transaction, known as the "Donation of Pepin," formed the legal foundation of the Republic of St. Peter, also known as the Papal States. Aistulf's signature in the Treaty of Pavia, wherein he surrendered all Lombard-conquered lands to the Roman Catholic Church, was what tightened the bow and made the whole thing official.

Exactly 90 years later, a mob of Muslim Arab marauders – or as they were known by the Europeans, the "Saracens" – infiltrated the borders of Rome. They were still riding on the adrenaline from having recently seized Sicily, and were now determined to get their hands on the rest of the peninsula. Throughout the city, they raised hell, swiping treasures from the churches they destroyed and slashing throats left and right. One of the raiders' greatest hauls came from the basilicas of St. Peter and St. Paul, for they lay just outside the defensive walls erected by Emperors Aurelian and Probus back in the 3rd century. The Church took a debilitating hit, for they lost entire vaults brimming with "rich liturgical vessels and jeweled relics." The one-of-a-kind silver table from Charlemagne, which bore a flawlessly detailed picture of Constantinople carved onto its surface, along with a gilded cross prised from the top of a Byzantine tomb, were among the most prized items of the booty. Even worse, the Saracens had vandalized the tombs of 2 of Rome's most beloved saints.

Distraught by the paralyzing loss, Pope Leo IV, whose coronation came a year after, funded the repairs and enhancements for the city's walls, as well as the reconstruction of 15 towers. At the same time, he authorized the construction of a fence of walls that surrounded the basilicas, enclosing Vatican Hill for the very first time. By 852, construction was complete. The walls, which were 12 feet thick, towered over the city at a height of 40 feet. In the years that followed, the Church planted their own watchtowers and bell towers by the walls, establishing their own fortified complex. Under the leadership of Pope Eugene III in the 12th century, the Vatican and Lateran both housed an arsenal and a weapon manufacturing facility.

In 1277, Pope Nicholas III built an elevated passageway that linked Vatican City to Castel Sant'Angelo, a sister fortress located to the east of the Tiber River. The secret corridor, named the *"Passetto di Borgo,"* ran about 2,600 feet in length and was designed to trick the naked eye into believing that it was just another hollow stretch of a defensive wall. In 1492, Pope Alexander VI, the infamous Rodrigo Borgia, expanded the passage by transforming the old walkway into a gallery and stacking an extra-long corridor above it. Torches lit up the slender corridor, and the pope's coat of arms, which showed a pair of overlapping keys, a bear, and the papal crown, were stamped onto the walls.

The *Passetto* served as emergency escape route for the popes. 2 years after the expansion, Pope Alexander VI used the corridor to flee from French raiders. Later, during the Sack of Rome in 1527, Pope Clement VII succeeded in dodging 20,000 of Emperor Charles V's rebel soldiers with the aid of the *Passetto*.

In 1279, Pope Nicholas IV decided to leave the Lateran Palace and relocate to the Vatican, where he broke tradition by establishing his papal residence there. He, too, boxed his new residence in with a line of defensive walls. Taking pride in his stunning new home, the pope tasked himself with embellishing the grounds within the walls. He planted a vibrant orchard *(pomerium)*, a radiant garden *(viridarium)*, and a lush square of manicured lawn *(pratellum)*, creating a breathtaking sanctuary for himself, where he could meditate in the company of nature.

Pope Nicholas IV

The pope had other ideas up his sleeves, but the beautifying of the Vatican would have to wait.

Schisms, Reconciliation, and Resurgence

"It is necessary to keep one's compass in one's eyes and not in the hand, for the hands execute, but the eye judges." – attributed to Michelangelo

A perfect storm would rear its ugly head at the turn of the 14th century. Between 1294 and 1303, the infamous Pope Boniface VIII entered a turbulent feud with the French King Philip IV. The pair had never gotten along, for the pope viewed Philip as rash and insubordinate, whereas the other was convinced that the pope was nothing but a money-starved and power-hungry crook hiding in holy clothing. Boniface was already disliked by not just the French authorities, but his own people, for his dishonest governing tactics, such as the sanctioning of simony (profiting from pardons, a seat in papal office, and other ecclesiastical privileges). He truly lost the public with his vocal advocacy of papal authority. Plainly put, Boniface asserted that apart from the papacy holding supreme dominion over spiritual matters in Europe, all political affairs should fall under the jurisdiction of the Roman Catholic Church, too.

Pope Boniface VIII

In 1296, Boniface decreed that all secular rulers request his permission first before applying new taxes to their lands. Few were pleased, but even fewer were bold enough to step out of line. Among these rebels was King Philip IV of France, who went ahead and taxed the clergy in his lands anyway, as he was in dire need of fattening up his treasury for an upcoming war against England. An enraged Boniface retaliated with a letter stating that all those who followed in the footsteps of Philip, or paid these illegal taxes, would be immediately excommunicated from the Church. When Philip responded by threatening to withhold all French profits geared towards Rome, Boniface shied away from his bluff and sat on his hands.

The back-and-forth bickering continued for some time, but things only escalated when Boniface published the *Unam Sanctum* in 1302. This papal bull, often said to be one of the most "extreme statements" ever made by the papacy, specified that "every human creature [was] subject to the Roman pontiff." In the same breath, he severed all ties with Philip and declared him excommunicated from the Church. Troops dispatched by an infuriated Philip proceeded to slap Boniface around, which traumatized the pope so much that he died a month later.

It would seem as if Boniface's death would have calmed things down, but the situation only went from bad to worse. Pope Benedict XI, Boniface's successor, ruled for roughly 9 months before his untimely death, which may or may not have been caused by poisoning on Philip's behalf. After a particularly tense papal conclave – the conference of bishops that convened to elect a new pope – the French-born Clement V was elected, a decision that incited outrage among the Roman Catholic masses. Fearing for his safety, Clement chose to stay behind in France and built his own papal residence in Avignon, launching the Avignon Papacy. From 1309-1377, Clement, along with the 6 popes that followed him, deserted the Roman offices and held their offices in Avignon.

Pope Clement V

After almost 7 decades in France with the papacy's strings pulled by the French royals, Pope Gregory XI reestablished the papal residence in the Vatican. That said, the homecoming did not sit well with French authorities, nor did it fare well among his own cardinals. At the time of his death in March of 1378, 6 of his cardinals were still stationed in Avignon, and they refused to budge. The papal conclave that decided Gregory's descendant was even more treacherous than Clement's. Romans feared that another French pope would be elected, so much so that a rabble of rioters protested outside and broke into the conclave to object. In the end, Pope Urban VI, an Italian-born cardinal who served a stint at Avignon, was elected.

Alas, Urban's uncompromising and disciplinarian-style leadership, as well as his failure to play well with the other cardinals set the stage for the Western Schism. The cardinals schemed behind his back and selected Antipope Clement VII to drive Urban out of his papal throne. When Clement VII could not conquer Rome in 1379, he set up camp in Avignon once more, splitting the Church and its people in half under the leadership of 2 competing popes. Most of the German

Empire and England supported Urban, whereas France, Castile, and Scotland sided with the antipope, further deepening the divide.

Multiple attempts were made to end the schism, the most pivotal of them being the Council of Pisa. Though the goal of the council was to find common ground and cease the split, an even greater rift was produced by the end of the meeting. There was now a 3rd pope in the picture – the Pisan Antipope.

Surprisingly, it would be Pisan Antipope John XXIII who led to the conclusion of this entire ordeal by calling for the Council of Constance, which was held between 1414 and 1418. By the end of the council, John, along with Avignon's Antipope Benedict XIII, were deposed, and Roman Pope Gregory XII tendered his resignation. The council then elected Martin V, the first pope to be embraced by the entire Church in 4 decades.

With the absence of the papacy in Rome, the city lay in shambles. Paint was peeling, doors were hanging on their last hinges, and entire churches and chapels were abandoned. The Vatican was in such disarray that even wild animals roamed free throughout the shell of the papal complex, including the alternative palace Pope Symmachus had built back in the 5th century. Passersby often saw cows munching away on Pope Nicholas's once-precious lawns. Wolves also frequented the area, unearthing and gorging on bodies. The Lateran Palace was in no better shape, for it had been badly marred by 2 fires in the previous century. The Vatican was in serious need of a makeover.

In 1447, Pope Nicholas V knocked down Eugene III's fortifications to make room for what is now called the "Apostolic Palace," or simply the "Vatican Palace," which continues to serve as the chief papal residence and headquarters to this day. Soon after, a prefect was chosen and charged with the supervision and maintenance of the palace. This was a position that lasted only until the 19th century, when the Church treasury found its pockets a little lighter than usual. As a means of cutting costs, an unsalaried committee was created in its place.

Gaspard Miltiade's picture of the Apostolic Palace

Pope Nicholas V

Construction of the palace was a project that dragged on for the next century-and-a-half. The hard hat was passed on to Pope Sixtus V, Pope Urban VII, and so forth, until Pope Pius XI finished it off with a museum entrance and an art gallery. On top of its museum, the palace today houses administrative offices, papal apartments, and a selection of private and public chapels.

One of the most notable additions to the palace was the Vatican library, which was sponsored by Pope Sixtus IV at the peak of the Renaissance. The vision of a public learning center open to all scholars was said to have been Nicholas's idea, but it was Sixtus who turned the vision into reality. The scribing and printing industries were booming in Europe, with illumination and scribing techniques more streamlined and refined than ever. This made the opening day of the library that much more significant.

Pope Sixtus IV

Pope Nicholas himself accumulated an "ornate library of old and new codices," and hoarded up to 3,000 volumes, many of them Greek and other European works translated into Latin. Sixtus, along with succeeding popes, added onto that collection, and later constructed the shelter for the manuscripts, books, and secret archives within the palace, dubbing it the "Palatine Library." The library came complete with new shelves, tables, benches, and printing presses. Pope Julius II and Pope Sixtus V would later pour vast sums of money into renovations and expansions for the library, revamping it with brand-new furniture, expensive artwork, and frescoed walls. It would not take long for the library to emerge as Europe's primary hub for ecclesiastical and non-ecclesiastical intellectuals alike.

What ensued can best be summed up as a golden age for the Vatican. Around the same time the idea of the library was conceived, Pope Sixtus IV hired Giovanni de Dolci to construct a special chapel within the Apostolic Palace. This was none other than the legendary 3-story Sistine Chapel, one of the most common images that springs to mind when one hears mention of the Vatican.

In 1507, an irritated Pope Julius II paced back and forth as he stared down a glaring crack fracturing the starry sky of the Sistine Chapel. When he could stand the eyesore no longer, he yanked an unamused Michelangelo out of a project in Florence and ordered him to paint over the battered ceiling. Michelangelo gawked at the task literally hovering over him, and when he finally located his words, he politely, but staunchly refused. Not only was he a strict sculptor by trade, he had only been exposed to the fresco technique once several years ago, and was rusty at best. Although Michelangelo usually relished challenges, Vasari suggests he was reluctant to work on the Sistine Chapel: "Michelangelo tried every means to avoid it, and recommended Raphael, for he saw the difficulty of the work, knew his lack of skill in coloring, and wanted to finish the tomb."

Instead, Michelangelo suggested Raphael, another renowned Italian painter 8 years his junior. Rejection was a foreign concept to the highly-strung Julius, who stubbornly maintained that no one but Michelangelo was allowed near his precious ceiling. Some theorized that the whispers of Raphael and architect Donato Bramante, whom many believed to be Michelangelo's artistic opponents, were what influenced the pope's decision-making. If the story is to be believed, Raphael and Bramante, who were well-aware of Michelangelo's lack of experience with frescoes, hoped to see him brought to his knees by the impossible task. They hoped that a humiliated Michelangelo would be traumatized by the failure enough that it would drive him out of Rome, leaving an abundance of work they could pick and choose from to their liking.

After a tense back-and-forth, Michelangelo finally caved and agreed to give the project a whirl, which he started in early 1508. With a canvas stretching 5,808 sq ft in size, 19% larger than a modern basketball court, Michelangelo had his work cut out for him. The mounting stress was made worse by the helicopter-styled supervision of Pope Julius II, who was not just demanding, but rigidly opinionated. Julius wanted a collage of paintings starring the 12 apostles, which was to be finished off with "filler decorations."

Nonetheless, Michelangelo stood his ground and held firm to his belief that the grand ceiling was deserving of something much more spectacular. Julius, having evidently met his match in the debate arena, ultimately granted the first-time professional painter permission to do with the ceiling as he wished. The moment the song of his muses drifted into his ears, Michelangelo put pen to paper and crafted a diagram for the ceiling, including plans for the 16 lunettes and an assortment of ornamental medallions. What materialized was a fantastic, but formidable plan illustrating the dark history of pre-saved humanity before the coming of Christ, one that would see the creation of over 300 individual figures.

Though Julius had promised to leave the tortured artist to his own accord, the impatient pope amped up the frequency of his visits in 1510. Julius was ecstatic with what he saw and often led his friends on private tours for a sneak peek of Michelangelo's work, but he was vexed by the painter's progress. At this point, half the ceiling was still empty space, but Julius decided to reopen the chapel doors. When Michelangelo objected, the pope allegedly shot back with the following threat: "If you do not take down the scaffold, I will have you thrown off it." Backed into a corner, Michelangelo obliged, dismantled the scaffold, and stood by until Julius achieved his fix with the first tours. In January of 1511, Michelangelo re-assembled the scaffold and returned to work.

At long last, on October 31, 1512, which racked up to a grand total of 54 months, Michelangelo, along with Pope Julius II and a crowd practically bursting at the seams with anticipation, was invited into the Sistine Chapel to see the finished ceiling for the very first time. As the congregation filed into the chapel, their eyes swiveling up in unison, a stupefied hush fell over them. The ceiling was tenfold more phenomenal than anyone could have imagined.

Adria Pingstone's picture of the Sistine Chapel

The Sistine Chapel ceiling

    The Sistine Chapel stands as a foremost example of High Renaissance art. The geometric, almost kaleidoscopic rhythms of the composition cohere with the Renaissance emphasis on mathematics and geometric calculus. The ceiling is remarkably complex with regard to both the actual narrative content and the artistic form, and the massive scope makes it difficult to approach as a viewer. To this end, the *Sistine Chapel* ceiling subverted the norms of spectatorship. In his study of the work, Charles Seymour noted, "Ever since its unveiling in 1512, the ceiling has also proved to generations of awed observers a visual puzzle of no small dimension. How was it ever meant actually to be seen? *All at one time?* If not, how and where should one begin to look? And then, how should one proceed? Finally, short of finding an inevitably uncomfortable spot on which to recline on the marble-incrusted pavement of the Chapel, where may one discover the best available point of viewing?"

    Running down the middle of the ceiling were 9 symbolic stories from the Bible, including The

Temptation, The Expulsion from the Garden, Jonah, and The Flood. Nude men and women, known as ignudi, were peppered into the frames of the scenes, and were said to represent mankind's strife before the arrival of Christ. Almost all of the ignudi men can be spotted posing with acorns. This was a subtle nod to his patron, whose family name, Rovere, translates to "oak" in Italian.

Without a doubt, the most recognizable of these pieces, which is still highly relevant in pop culture to this day, was the Creation of Adam. The Creation of Adam, which was placed right next to the Creation of Eve, was seated in the center panel of the ceiling. In this scene, God is shown as a muscular, older man sporting white robes with silvery locks and a flowing beard. The divine figure is nestled in the interlocking embrace of an army of wingless angels, and is seen leaning forward with his arm and forefinger extended. Just a breath away from God's finger was the limp hand of a naked Adam, casually lounging upon a rock on his elbow with one of his legs propped up. If one were to take a closer look, a fair-haired female figure can be also be spotted peering out from under God's arm, which historians believe to be Eve.

Creation of Adam

In addition to the Sistine Chapel, Pope Julius II would pick up where Nicholas V had left off and restart the repairs on the Old St. Peter's Basilica in 1503. Donato Bramante was commissioned to tear down, redesign, and rebuild a whole new basilica in its place, later shedding the "Old" from its name. The refurbished basilica, shaped as a triple-aisled Latin cross, now hosted a splendid tomb for Julius and St. Peter, Michelangelo's spectacular white stone dome right above the shrine, and a seating capacity of 20,000 and 60,000 standing. It rose to prominence as the largest church of its time, and due to its size and extravagance, was the fixed setting for all official papal ceremonies and Christian celebrations. Also found in the basilica was a cloister for monks, complete with a dazzling garden and an ornamented fountain in its center.

Alves Gaspar's picture of the main façade and dome of St. Peter's Basilica

Construction of the basilica would only be completed in 1656. To top it all off, Gian Lorenzo Bernini was tasked with developing what was later called the "Piazza of St. Peter," or "St. Peter's Square." Despite its name, the square was elliptical, given its shape by 284 colonnades and 88 pilasters, and could hold up to 400,000 people on a good day. The trapezoid in front of the basilica was attached to the semi-circular colonnades, reminiscent of an old-fashioned keyhole from above. 140 statues of popes, martyrs, and other Catholic figures designed by Bernini and his students were perched on top of the colonnades. Caligula's obelisk was later placed in the center of the square.

Andreas Tille's picture of the square

In 1506, Julius decided to fill the void between the chapel and Pope Innocent VIII's Villa Belvedere with a courtyard, and he hired Bramante once again for the job. The distinguished courtyard, which was named the *"Cortile del Belvedere"* (Belvedere Courtyard), boasted 3 levels that were connected by stylish stairwells, and open-air walkways bound by columns and high arches. Towards the end of the 16th century, the Belvedere Courtyard was halved in 2 to create space for a new wing for the library. Today, the Belvedere Courtyard is joined by 2 other courtyards within the vicinity – the Library Courtyard, and the Pigna Courtyard. The Pigna, located on the northern neck of the complex, was named after the 4-meter tall bronze pinecone sitting in the atrium of the Old St. Peter's Basilica. A set of bronze peacocks stood on either side of the pinecone.

That same year, Julius invited their papal allies, more precisely, the Swiss Cantons of Helvetian descent, to Rome. As one writer put it, the Helvetian mercenaries were "a people of warriors, famous for their valor of soldiers." At the time, around 15,000 Swiss mercenaries were eligible for employment. Their government, the modest Confederation of Cantons, permitted their men to enlist in Julius' private army in return for salt, corn, and other rare and valuable commodities.

On January 22, 1506, 150 Swiss soldiers, directed by Captain Kasparvon Silenen, marched into the Vatican, where they were blessed by Julius. The force was small, but consisted of Swiss military elites. They were charged with guarding the Apostolic Palace and the Vatican in general, as well as keeping the pope safe.

The soldiers, known as the Pontifical Swiss Guards, were equipped with broadswords, halberds (spear and battleaxe hybrids), and other top-of-the-line Swiss weaponry. They donned a white cross, a symbol of the Swiss, and the papal coat of arms on the chests of their armors. In 1512, they were presented with the title of "Defenders of the Church's Freedom." Some say they were forefathers of modern day special forces. In the early 19th century, the pontifical army was enlarged by Pope Pius VII's Italian-born Corps of Gendarmes.

Often recognized as the most important of all Pontifical Guard military engagements was their role as the Vatican's defense during the 1527 Sack of Rome. Only 42 of the 189 guards were left standing, for these were the ones who had accompanied Pope Clement VII to safety through the *Passetto*. The remaining 147, along with 200 others, lost their lives defending papal property on the steps of the basilica. The Vatican experienced déjà vu when pillagers violated the tombs of popes and saints, in the end making off with loot worth 10 million ducats.

The Pontifical Swiss Guards continue to serve the Vatican today, and now average a number of about 130 in service at any given time. All candidates for the position were required to be Catholic, unmarried Swiss citizens with backgrounds in the Swiss military. A height limit has been set at 5'8", and the age limit between 19 and 30. As a Swiss Guard, one was expected to be of "impeccable moral and religious character." Most importantly, one had to be prepared to die for the pope. One can still see them posted around the Vatican, dressed in their traditional blue-and-gold striped uniforms, and the iconic bright tufts of red feathers on their helmets, halberds in hand.

Alberto Luccaroni's picture of Swiss Guards

Too Many Cooks in the Kitchen

"Faith is a living, daring confidence in God's grace, so sure and certain that a man could stake his life on it a thousand times." – attributed to Martin Luther

The bases and captured territories of the Papal States also multiplied between the 15th and 16th centuries. For this the Church was indebted to Pope Julius II, whose alternative monikers were the "Warrior Pope" and the "Fearsome Pope." Apart from being an avid patron of the arts, Julius was a fierce general who led the Pontifical Guards in several successful military campaigns in defense of the papacy, albeit besmirching the name of the Church along the way. With the help of the League of Cambrai – an alliance between the Pope, Emperor Maximilian I, Spanish King Ferdinand II, and other Italian states – the papal republic acquired the Italian city of Bologna, the Umbrian Perugia, Cervia, and Faenza, among others. The Papal States also recaptured Ravenna, Rimini, and other territories appropriated by Venice.

At this stage, the Vatican was a powerhouse that did not appear to be slowing down anytime soon, but even with all the progress made in the 1500s, the Vatican drifted into troubled waters about midway into the 16th century. For starters, the reputation of the Church drastically decayed in the public eye, no thanks to the rampant promotion and hawking of plenary indulgences within the holy community. In essence, plenary indulgences were monetary or material gifts presented to the Church in exchange for the complete forgiveness of sins, as well as a guaranteed seat in Heaven.

Others were sickened by Pope Sixtus IV and the Church's gross involvement in the nightmarish Spanish Inquisition, a gory persecution of heretics that officially claimed between 3,000 and 5,000 lives. Even more distressing was the Church's treatment of those who had differing opinions on Catholic norms. Even scholars like English philosopher John Wycliffe, Geralomo Savonarola, and John Huss, who had a few choice words to say about the phenomena of purgatory, relic-worshiping, and so forth, were dealt with violently. Most notably, the latter 2 were burned alive at the stakes.

On top of the papacy's brazen corruption, the Scientific Revolution that unfolded in Europe bred a new generation of inquisitive, out-of-the-box thinkers. As such, more and more of these minds, which swayed towards science, logic, and reason, detached themselves from the Church. One of the most recognizable names and founders of the Reformation movement was Martin Luther. In 1517, Luther penned an academically formatted letter of protest objecting to the sale of the indulgences and other Church corruptions, which he entitled the "95 Theses." He then had the document translated to Latin, pinned the document to the door of the Catholic Castle Church in Wittenberg, and produced pamphlets that were then distributed to the German Christians.

Luther

It would not be long before he amassed his own followers, thus creating the Protestant Church. The Protestants slammed and denounced several Catholic concepts to separate themselves from the herd, such as the Catholic's worshiping of Mary, Communion and other sacraments, the celibacy of clergymen, and boldest of all – the extent of papal authority. 3 days into January of 1521, Pope Leo X published the papal bull, *Decet Romanum Pontificem*, eternally banning Luther from the Catholic Church. 3 months later, Luther was branded a criminal and blasphemer by Holy Roman Emperor Charles V.

A little over a decade later, the Roman Catholic Church entered another troubling chapter with the emergence of the English Reformation. King Henry VIII of England longed to part ways with his wife, Catherine of Aragon. His eyes had not only wandered to his mistress, Anne Boleyn, he resented Catherine for her failure to produce a male heir to the throne. By 1527, the 42-year-old Catherine had become barren, solidifying the king's decision for a divorce. However, under the Catholic Church, divorce was out of the question, as only the widowed were permitted to take new partners.

Henry weighed out the pros and cons to the situation. If he decided to go through with the divorce, he faced excommunication from the Catholic Church. On the other hand, he wasn't getting any younger himself, so if he wished to prolong his bloodline, he needed a new wife, and fast.

Still, Henry tread lightly and applied for "papal dispensation," essentially a free pass from the Church's divorce laws, only to have his requests rejected one after another. By 1533, Henry could wait no longer. He circumvented the Church, convinced the Archbishop of Canterbury to grant him a divorce, and promptly took Boleyn as his wife. Just as Henry had anticipated, in December of that year, the pope published a bull and prohibited the English king from ever returning to the Catholic Church.

This, of course, gave rise to the Anglican Church of England. The bulk of the English public rejoiced at Henry's decision to split from the Roman church, for they, too, were fed up with the corrupt state of the Catholic churches based in England. They were tired of coughing up their hard-earned money for ridiculous fees, including baptisms and burials on holy grounds; the latter was the only other route one could take to the Pearly Gates. The sharpest sting of all was the Church's suspiciously flourishing treasury, criticized by the poor who stayed poor. In short order, a parliamentary act declared Henry the Supreme Head of the English church.

The rise of Pope Paul IV in 1555 did little to mend the tarnished image of the Roman Catholic Church. Paul, a learned man with excellent training in the languages of Greek, Hebrew, and Latin, had a burning thirst for reform, and he unleashed a series of rehabilitative laws designed to reorganize and straighten out the Church. However, many of these laws bordered or surpassed the lines of tyranny. His private police squads patrolled the churches 24/7 and were expected to report back to the papal offices with fully-ticked checklists and a list of miscreants. Monks missing from monasteries during "working hours" were imprisoned, and repeat offenders were sentenced to work as galley slaves. These were human chattels and convicts made to operate the oars of galleys and warships.

Pope Paul IV

In 1559, the Church more than dabbled in censorship when Paul released the first catalogue of banned literature entitled the "Index of Forbidden Books." Collaborating with the Congregation of the Inquisition, the Church targeted individuals in possession of dangerous literature and penalized them, sometimes so severely that they were locked away for years. Paul incurred the wrath of even more of his peers when he singled out 2 popular cardinals, Reginald Pole and Giovanni Morone, and accused them of sympathizing with the heretics.

Perhaps most galling of all to Europeans was Paul's hypocrisy. While he claimed to be an ardent supporter of reform, he neglected to use the Church's own tool for reform, the Council of Trent. Paul was himself later accused of nepotism, for he promoted his "unprincipled nephew," Carlo Carafa, to cardinal, and turned a blind eye when Carafa's antics proceeded to eat away at the fabric of the Church from within.

In July of 1555, the Church reawakened tensions with the Jewish community when Paul issued a bull called the *"Cum nimis absurdum."* As its name suggests, the bull contained a set of absurd laws and prejudiced restrictions aimed at the Jews. The same bull decreed that all Jews be rounded up and transported to a squalid neighborhood designated for the Jews known as the "Rome Ghetto." The pope believed it to be "completely senseless and inappropriate to be in a situation where Christian piety allows the Jews (whose guilt – all of their own doing – has condemned them to eternal slavery) access to our society, or even to live among us."

Paul's actions would also lead to hostilities with the Spanish King Philip II. Philip spurned Paul's demands for control of the Spanish kingdom, as these were cherished rights that his father, Roman Emperor Charles V, had bequeathed to him. Furthermore, Philip was convinced that he needed no help with Spanish governance – not only was heresy extinct in the mainland, thanks to the Inquisition, a predominantly Spanish operation, the influence of the Jews and the Moors had been successfully kept at bay. Against the advice of his peers, Paul entered a year-long war with Philip just a year later, which he eventually lost. His defeat was finalized in the 1557 Treaty of Cave, a document that ended the French and Vatican alliance, brokered peace between the Church and Spain, and declared the Italian town of Cave and other territories free from the papal republic.

Most of Paul's reforms might have appeared to have spoiled the chances of the papal republic's success in the long run, but the majority of the reforms actually had good intentions, and those that worked stuck around for awhile. Seminaries were created to provide better training for priests and other clergymen. The crackdowns on churches resulted in tightened rules and the return to simplistic living with a focus on spreading gospel and a commitment to charity.

Additionally, reforms brought about by the Council of Trent further improved the discipline within the Church. The clampdown on churches ensured a fixed and immovable budget, and that the elections of bishops for political and other immoral purposes ceased, or at the very least were kept to a minimum. The council then directed its focus to reinstating the importance of celibacy, then on halting absenteeism. Bishops could no longer lounge around in their summer villas, and were now required to live within the premises of their assigned dioceses.

Regardless of the Church's troubles, the Papal States continued to grow. In 1598, Pope Clement VIII succeeded in reeling in the Duchy of Ferrara, and in 1631, the Vatican reclaimed the Duchy of Urbino. At its height in the 18th century, the Papal States controlled most of central Italy, including the territories of Umbria, Marche, Latium, the northern lands of the Romagna, and Pontecorvo and Benevento in the southern tip of the country. The Comtat Venaissin, which marked the area outside the city of Avignon, was also part of papal territory.

Clash of the Republics, the Risorgimento, and the Modern Day Vatican

"If a future pope teaches anything contrary to the Catholic faith, do not follow him." –

attributed to Pope Pius IX

It would seem as if the basilica at the Vatican was cursed, for it fell victim to yet another fire in 1823. The wayward flames of the uncontrollable fire swept across the twice-renovated St. Peter's Basilica, consuming its glamorous gilded mosaic floors and irreplaceable marble columns. An unknown, but pitifully large number of paintings, statues, and other artworks featuring popes, saints, and biblical figures, were also devoured by the flames. Though the fire was quelled the next evening, there was tremendous and lasting damage. The following day, a mournful Pope Leo XII arranged an emergency meeting with top-tier cardinals and whipped up a speech addressed to the entire Catholic congregation around the world. In it, the pope recounted the events of the fire, emphasized what had been lost in the disaster, and enlisted the public's help in piecing the basilica back together. The idea was to build an identical model of the fallen basilica by incorporating columns, walls, floor tiles, and other pieces that survived the fire. New sections of the church would be refashioned from the same materials.

Thus, for the next 2 decades, charred chunks of the church were razed to the ground or restored. Artists were hired to recreate lost sculptures and the frescoes on the walls. Staff installed recovered artifacts and new art pieces.

The plea to restore one of the Vatican's greatest treasures was not heard by just the Catholics, but sympathetic souls around the globe. Russia's Tsar Nicholas I donated raw piles of malachite and lapis lazuli blocks, which came in handy in recreating the altars found in both wings of the cross-shaped church. Egyptian royals pitched in on the effort, too; King Fouad I gifted handmade columns and windows made from alabaster, a milky, off-white mineral used primarily for the construction of ornaments and decorative structures.

Fortunately, there were quite a few items the basilica's staff succeeded in saving from the flames. Among the most valuable relics found buried beneath the rubble was a short, rusty link of a chain that was said to have been used on St. Paul during one of his many stays in the Roman jails. The chain is now enclosed in a glass box and can be seen on display on the altar above his tomb. Another was a 12th century Easter candle marble sculpture. The remarkable pillar stood over 18 feet in height and was partitioned in 8 sections like a totem pole. In place of brightly-colored totems and faces, it featured intricate carvings of complex Biblical scenes.

The basilica's Chapel of Relics, which still stands today, exhibits a varying range of artifacts collected throughout the centuries, including the encased fingernails, bone, and skull fragments of popes and saints. Another case displays a hunk of wood said to come from the Basilica di Santa Croce (Sacred Cross) in Jerusalem, derived from the very cross that Christ was nailed on. Other surviving items include a 12th century chandelier, as well as St. Paul's marble tombstone. About a century later, 150 new columns were added to the porch at the entrance.

December 10, 1854, marked the day the doors of the basilica reopened. Pope Pius IX consecrated the church with a grand ceremony, joined by hundreds of cardinals, bishops, and priests from around the world. Owing to the efforts made by the restoration staff, visitors could once again experience the enchanting beauty within the basilica. Soon after, St. Peter's Basilica was declared a national monument.

Like an old onion, the Vatican kept all the gleam of its shiny, smooth exterior, but its moist, mushy layers were slowly rotting away from within. Pope Gregory XVI, the 252nd and last monk-turned-pope, was another tough leader that his peers found hard to swallow. The austere and inflexible environment of the Benedictine Camaldolese community he was raised in seeped into his style of governance, and his intolerant, ultra-conservative opinions were views the people could not tolerate.

Pope Gregory XVI

To be fair, the bridge the Church had built over troubled waters not only bore cracks like veins under translucent skin, it was standing on its last leg. At this point, the throats of rioters pining for democracy and protesters calling for the separation of church and state had already turned dry and scratchy. Needless to say, when Gregory, a hardcore traditionalist who opposed all liberal views other than slavery, was elected, all hell broke loose. On February 3, an unruly mob attacked and ran the Duke of Modena from the papal-owned Mantua out of town. The next day, a swarm of Bolognese insurgents stormed into government offices, their cries for freedom heard throughout the country.

Be that as it may, Gregory's reign was not without its upside. With the 200 new missionaries he personally appointed, along with the 70 new dioceses and vicarships established under his rule, the number of global Catholic missions soared. He moonlighted as an art patron and added the Egyptian and Etruscan exhibits to the Vatican Museums. Sadly, his overeager and costly art contributions, not to mention his careless military-related expenses, exhausted the Vatican treasury, which only served to further intensify the people's contempt for him.

The 1846 Papal Conclave on the 14th of June, which commenced 13 days after Gregory's death, was among the most momentous of all the papal elections. The 50 members from the College of Cardinals who gathered at the Quirinal Palace that day felt the pressure of the public's eyes searing into their backs. They were tasked with choosing not just the head of the Catholic Church, their vote determined the Sovereign Ruler who would govern the fragile Papal States.

The voters were split down the middle. On one side, there were the hardliner conservatives who supported Gregory's papacy, and fought for "papal absolutism." Their pick was Gregory's own Secretary of State, Cardinal Luigi Lambruschini. On the other end of the spectrum, the liberal cardinals pushed for moderate reform, which they hoped would come with their leading candidate, Cardinal Giovanni Maria Mastai-Ferretti.

After much debate, the cardinals settled on Mastai-Ferretti on the 16th, after he received 4 votes more than the majority rule. Conservative Catholic monarchs and clergymen from all levels of society who were displeased with the results stepped forward to voice their discontent in the hopes of vetoing the cardinal, but what was done was done. When Austrian Emperor Ferdinand got wind of the election results, he sent the Archbishop of Milan, Karl Gaisruck, to reverse the situation. To the emperor's dismay, by the time Gaisruck stumbled through the doors of the palace, Feretti, now Pope Pius IX, had already been crowned.

For the first half of Pius' rule, the approval ratings for the papacy spiked, and were the highest they had ever been in decades. Pius kept his word and introduced a smart set of "moderate reforms," such as the building of new agricultural buildings and the updating of farming technology in the Vatican and other papal territories. He freed all political prisoners and awarded them amnesty, which irritated the conservative characters of the French and Austrian monarchs. He then revoked all laws that made it compulsory for Jews and non-Christians to attend Christian services, and one-upped his predecessors by opening papal-funded charities in Jewish communities.

Taking the ongoing criticisms of the Church's spending habits into account, Pius established a finance committee composed of 4 cardinals that would handle the budgets of the states' 20 provinces. He poured money into the improvement of infrastructure, repaving roads, repairing seaports, patching up bridges and aqueducts, and finally, establishing a railway line that linked all the Papal States in northern Italy. To motivate production in the local industries, he offered "papal prizes" to those that surpassed set goals. He even joined forces with the Protestant Church to build a law school in Rome dedicated to the training of mediators and the study of international conflict resolution.

For all of Pius's efforts, it would not take long for the public's faith in him to wane. Critics crawling out of the woodwork accused him of faking his liberalism, and insisted that he was a conservative reactionary at heart. The offices of the Papal States were inundated with complaints from those who had a bone to pick with what they regarded as their faulty justice system. The public blasted the papal government for its inability to keep proper records and legal books, and questioned the equity and competence of the Church's judges. Not only were 133 people put to death under Pius' dominion, the holy government failed to fend off the gangs that constantly harassed business owners throughout the Papal States.

In the end, it would only be in 1848 that Pius truly lost all hope of liberal support. The pope's subjects hoped that Pius would unify Italy. Only, to do so, the papacy would have to declare war against Catholic Austria, whose monarchs staunchly refused to surrender their territories in the northern part of Italy. As much as their sentiments resonated with him, they were not enough to move him into caving into their wishes. He stood his ground, and announced that he would not mobilize the Vatican guards.

It was then that radical Italian liberals decided they had no choice but to turn to their last resort – violence. In mid-November that year, Pius's Prime Minister, Pellegrino Rossi, had a knife plunged into his neck on the front steps of the Parliament building. As the Pontifical Guards combated the armed rioters in the days that followed, Pius attempted to flee, but he was detained by the raiders, with the help of the Italian troops, thereby making him a "Prisoner in the Vatican."

The Italian government reputedly engaged in negotiations with Pius. They worked on persuading him to give up authority over the Papal States, and at one point, even offered to let him keep Leonine City west of the Tiber River, to which Pius refused. A few weeks after the Italian troops marched into Rome, seizing all properties apart from the Apostolic Palace, the Roman citizens finally relented and voted to join Italy.

This 19th century campaign for Italian unification, which eventually led to the rise of the Kingdom of Italy in 1861, was known as the "*Risorgimento.*" In 1870, the remaining papal territories were acquired by Italian King Victor Emmanuel II, who then named Rome the capital of his kingdom. Pius died 8 years later.

The next year, the pope's temporal (non-spiritual) powers were rescinded. In 1895, Roma Catholicism was no longer the official religion of Italy, which put an end to all obligatory religious studies in public schools. Tax exemptions were also granted to institutions of all religions.

All that was left of the Papal States' territories were the lands of the Vatican, including the Villa of Castel Gandolfo and the palaces of the Lateran, but the Church would not stand for it, resulting in a continuing feud that lasted for the next 6 decades. Until 1929, 4 popes – Leo XIII, Pius X, Benedict XV, and Pius XI, respectively – called themselves the Prisoners of the Vatican, and placed themselves under house arrest in protest against the new Italian kingdom. Like Pius IX, the protesting popes claimed that the "anticlerical" Italian state had robbed the papal empire, and hoped that their actions would be enough to reverse the verdict, but in the end, all their efforts were futile.

On February 11, 1929, the dispute finally came to a close. The document, entitled the "Lateran Treaty," was signed by Benito Mussolini for the Italian government, and secretary of the Patrimony of St. Peter, Cardinal Pietro Gasparri, on behalf of the papacy. Under the terms of the treaty, the papacy recognized Italy as its own state, and agreed to keep their hands off Rome, for it was now the Italian capital. In return, Mussolini declared that all 109 acres of Vatican City would now be under sole jurisdiction of the papacy, and granted the area its independence. As of June 7, 1929, the Vatican became its own independent nation. What was more, the Church was given $92 million to reimburse them for the loss of the Papal States.

In January of 1959, the Vatican made headlines around the world once more when Pope John XXIII created the Ecumenical Council Vatican II (or simply "Vatican II," for short). News of the council astounded Catholics around the globe, for it was the first of its kind in close to a century. As Reverend John O'Malley, a professor from Georgetown University, put it, "Many people maintained that with the definition of papal infallibility in 1870, councils were no longer needed. So it was a big surprise." The Vatican II, which transpired between 1962 and 1965, was not only open to the 2,500 bishops and cardinals it invited, the council welcomed laymen and laywomen from near and far. Pope John felt it necessary for the Church to regroup, for the heartache and suffering caused by World War II were still taking a toll across the globe.

The new policies, which were centered on reconciliation, set out to modernize the Church. Catholics were encouraged to build new bridges with what they previously viewed as rival faiths. They were to pray, celebrate, and partner with other Christian factions so they could more efficiently spread God's word. The council agreed to lighten their grasp around media censorship, and proposed new reforms aimed at education. To better appeal to those ignorant of the gospel in faraway places, Masses could now be conducted in any language.

Today, there are roughly 600 people who reside in the smallest country in the world, but most of them live "abroad." Over 23 of the 44-hectare space is made up of the Vatican gardens. Apart from its beautiful churches, marvelous museums, and ancient ruins, the miniature country is home to an observatory, a pharmacy, and a medley of hotels nearby. As of 2011, reports show that more than 5 million tourists flock to Vatican City each year, with 25,000 of them squeezed into tiny space on the daily, each one more eager than the last to experience the magical, historic beauty of the home of the Roman Catholic Church.

Online Resources

Other Catholic history titles by Charles River Editors & Sean McLachlan

Other titles about the Vatican on Amazon

Bibliography

Editors, History Channel. "VATICAN CITY." *History Channel*. A&E Television Networks, LLC, 2016. Web. 3 July 2017. <http://www.history.com/topics/vatican-city>.

Klein, Christopher. "10 Things You May Not Know About the Vatican." *History Channel Stories*. A&E Television Networks, LLC, 12 Mar. 2013. Web. 3 July 2017. <http://www.history.com/news/10-things-you-may-not-know-about-the-vatican>.

Suddath, Claire. "Top 10 Vatican Pop-Culture Moments." *Time*. Time, Inc., 20 Oct. 2010. Web. 3 July 2017. <http://content.time.com/time/specials/packages/article/0,28804,2026525_2026524_2026523,00.html>.

Editors, Eternal City Education. "THE VATICAN BEFORE CHRISTIANITY." *Eternal City Education*. Eternal City Education, LLC, 26 Sept. 2013. Web. 3 July 2017. <http://eternalcityeducation.com/blog/vatican-christianity/>.

Editors, Vatican.Com. "The Vatican Hill." *Vatican.Com*. Internet Dominion Company, 26 June 2013. Web. 3 July 2017. <http://vatican.com/articles/info/the_vatican_hill-a4127>.

Baumgarten, Paul Maria. "The Vatican." *New Advent*. Robert Appleton Company, 1912. Web. 3 July 2017. <http://www.newadvent.org/cathen/15276b.htm>.

Scheifler, Michael. "What Does the Word Vatican Mean?" *Bible Light*. Bible Light, LLC, 2003. Web. 3 July 2017. <http://biblelight.net/vatican.htm>.

Woods, Stella. "The sacred site of Mons Vaticanus and its giant serpent." *Living Now*. Living Now Media, 9 Aug. 2013. Web. 3 July 2017. <https://livingnow.com.au/sacred-site-mons-vaticanus-giant-serpent/>.

Current, Ron. "The Circus of Roman Emperor Nero: Where St. Peter was martyred." *Still Current*. WordPress, 9 Nov. 2016. Web. 3 July 2017. <https://stillcurrent.wordpress.com/2016/11/09/the-circus-of-roman-emperor-nero-where-st-peter-was-martyred/>.

Editors, Rome Reborn. "Circus of Gaius and Nero." *Rome Reborn*. Rectors and Visitors of the University of Virginia, 2008. Web. 3 July 2017. <http://archive1.village.virginia.edu/spw4s/RomanForum/GoogleEarth/AK_GE/AK_HTML/AS-004.html>.

Editors, Revolvy. " Vatican City ." *Revolvy*. Revolvy, LLC, 3 July 2017. Web. 3 July 2017. <https://www.revolvy.com/topic/Vatican%20City&item_type=topic>.

Editors, Ancient Origins. "The Madness of Caligula." *Ancient Origins*. Novus Web Solutions, 29 Sept. 2014. Web. 3 July 2017. <http://www.ancient-origins.net/history-famous-people/madness-caligula-002132>.

Trueman, C. N. "Rome and Christianity." *The History Learning Site*. The History Learning Site, Ltd., 16 Mar. 2015. Web. 3 July 2017. <http://www.historylearningsite.co.uk/ancient-rome/rome-and-christianity/>.

Editors, Got Questions. "What were the different missionary journeys of Paul?" *Got Questions*. Got Questions Ministries, 2015. Web. 3 July 2017. <https://www.gotquestions.org/missionary-journeys-Paul.html>.

Editors, Got Questions. "What happened on Paul's first missionary journey?" *Got Questions*. Got Questions Ministries, 2015. Web. 3 July 2017. <https://www.gotquestions.org/Paul-first-missionary-journey.html>.

Editors, Got Questions. "What happened on Paul's second missionary journey?" *Got Questions*. Got Questions Ministries, 2015. Web. 3 July 2017. <https://www.gotquestions.org/Paul-second-missionary-journey.html>.

Wisniewski, J. "5 Ridiculous Lies You Believe About Ancient Civilizations." *Cracked*. Scripps Company, 7 July 2013. Web. 3 July 2017. <http://www.cracked.com/article_20536_5-ridiculous-lies-you-believe-about-ancient-civilizations.html>.

Malik, Shushma, and Caillan Davenport. "Mythbusting Ancient Rome – throwing Christians to the lions." *The University of Queensland*. The University of Queensland, 22 Nov. 2016. Web. 3 July 2017. <https://hapi.uq.edu.au/article/2016/11/mythbusting-ancient-rome-%E2%80%93-throwing-christians-lions>.

Editors, PBS. "The Great Fire of Rome Background." *PBS - Secrets of the Dead*. Thirteen Productions, LLC, 2013. Web. 3 July 2017. <http://www.pbs.org/wnet/secrets/great-fire-rome-background/1446/>.

Hays, Jeffrey. "CHRISTIANITY IN THE ROMAN EMPIRE." *Facts and Details*. Jeffrey Hays, 2013. Web. 3 July 2017.

<http://factsanddetails.com/world/cat56/sub368/item2079.html>.

Editors, Saylor. "Christianity and the Roman Empire." *Saylor*. The Saylor Foundation, 2014. Web. 3 July 2017. <https://www.saylor.org/site/wp-content/uploads/2012/10/HIST101-6.4.2-ChristianityAndTheRomanEmpire-FINAL1.pdf>.

Zavada, Jack. "What Is Agape?" *Thought Company*. Thought Company, Inc., 31 Mar. 2017. Web. 3 July 2017. <https://www.thoughtco.com/g00/agape-love-in-the-bible-700675?i10c.referrer=https%3A%2F%2Fwww.google.com.tw%2F>.

Johnson, Jennifer A. "Tattoos of the Cross." *Christianity Today*. Christianity Today, LLC, 19 Mar. 2009. Web. 3 July 2017. <http://www.christianitytoday.com/history/2009/march/tattoos-of-cross.html>.

Peach, David. "10 Famous Christian Martyrs." *What Christians Want to Know*. Telling Ministries, LLC, 11 Apr. 2017. Web. 3 July 2017. <http://www.whatchristianswanttoknow.com/10-famous-christian-martyrs/>.

Sherman, Elisabeth. "7 Astounding Stories Of Early Christian Martyrs' Brutal Deaths." *All That is Interesting*. All That is Interesting, Ltd., 16 Nov. 2016. Web. 4 July 2017. <http://all-that-is-interesting.com/christian-martyrs>.

Editors, Christian History Institute. "#107: CONSTANTINE'S VISION." *Christian History Institute*. Christian History Institute, 2017. Web. 4 July 2017. <https://www.christianhistoryinstitute.org/study/module/constantine/>.

Editors, Biography.Com. "Constantine I." *Biography.Com*. A&E Television Networks, LLC, 1 Apr. 2014. Web. 4 July 2017. <https://www.biography.com/people/constantine-l-39496>.

Editors, National Geographic. "Constantine the Great Rules." *National Geographic*. National Geographic Society, 2012. Web. 4 July 2017. <http://www.nationalgeographic.com/lostgospel/timeline_10.html>.

Editors, Biography Online. "Constantine The Great Biography." *Biography Online*. Biography Online, Ltd., 2011. Web. 4 July 2017. <http://www.biographyonline.net/military/constantine.html>.

Editors, Bible Study Tools. "The Tenth Persecution, Under Diocletian, A.D. 303." *Bible Study Tools*. Salem Web Network, 2015. Web. 4 July 2017. <http://www.biblestudytools.com/history/foxs-book-of-martyrs/the-tenth-persecution-under-diocletian-a-d-303.html>.

Editors, Religion Facts. "The Conversion of Constantine." *Religion Facts*. Religion Facts,

Ltd., 2008. Web. 4 July 2017. <http://www.religionfacts.com/conversion-of-constantine>.

Fairchild, Mary. "Roman Catholic Church History." *Thought Company*. Thought Company, Inc., 14 Mar. 2017. Web. 4 July 2017. <https://www.thoughtco.com/g00/roman-catholic-church-history-700528?i10c.referrer=https%3A%2F%2Fwww.google.com.tw%2F>.

MachLachlan, Sean. "The death of paganism: how the Roman Empire converted to Christianity." *Gadling*. Gadling, Inc., 21 Sept. 2010. Web. 4 July 2017. <http://gadling.com/2010/09/21/the-death-of-paganism-how-the-roman-empire-converted-to-christi/>.

Editors, Church Pop. "The Lost 1200-Year-Old Wonder: A Tour of the Old St. Peter's Basilica." *Church Pop*. Church Pop, Inc., 3 Aug. 2015. Web. 4 July 2017. <https://churchpop.com/2015/08/03/the-lost-1200-year-old-wonder-a-tour-of-the-old-st-peters-basilica/>.

Editors, Encyclopedia Britannica. "Old Saint Peter's Basilica." *Encyclopedia Britannica*. Encyclopedia Britannica, Inc., 29 July 2010. Web. 4 July 2017. <https://www.britannica.com/topic/Old-Saint-Peters-Basilica>.

Editors, Catholic Online. "History of Popes." *Catholic Online*. Catholic Online, LLC, 2010. Web. 4 July 2017. <http://www.catholic.org/pope/pope_slide.php>.

Cline, Austin. "Was Peter the First Pope?" *Thought Company*. Thought Company, Inc., 17 Mar. 2017. Web. 4 July 2017. <https://www.thoughtco.com/g00/was-peter-the-first-pope-250646?i10c.referrer=https%3A%2F%2Fwww.google.com.tw%2F>.

Editors, A View on Cities. "St. John Lateran." *A View on Cities*. A View on Cities, LLC, 2011. Web. 4 July 2017. <http://www.aviewoncities.com/rome/sangiovanniinlaterano.htm>.

Editors, Encylopedia.Com. "Papal States." *Encyclopedia.Com*. The Columbia University Press, 2011. Web. 4 July 2017. <http://www.encyclopedia.com/history/modern-europe/italian-history/papal-states>.

Editors, Encyclopedia Britannica. "Papal States." *Encyclopedia Britannica*. Encyclopedia Britannica, Inc., 15 Apr. 2015. Web. 4 July 2017. <https://www.britannica.com/place/Papal-States>.

Snell, Melissa. "The Origin and Decline of the Papal States." *Thought Company*. Thought Company, Inc., 15 Mar. 2017. Web. 5 July 2017. <https://www.thoughtco.com/g00/the-papal-states-1789449?i10c.referrer=https%3A%2F%2Fwww.google.com.tw%2F>.

Editors, Order of Constantine. "Constantine the Great 272 to 337 AD." *Order of Constantine the Great.* The Royal Order of Constantine the Great and Saint Helen, 2014. Web. 5 July 2017. <http://www.orderofconstantinethegreat.com/constantine_the_great.htm>.

Foresi, Tiffany. "'The absolute right to rule' – The Divine Right of Kings." *Royal Central.* Royal Central, Ltd., 25 Nov. 2014. Web. 5 July 2017. <http://royalcentral.co.uk/blogs/the-absolute-right-to-rule-the-divine-right-of-kings-40465>.

Editors, Encyclopedia Britannica. "Iconoclastic Controversy." *Encyclopedia Britannica.* Encyclopedia Britannica, Inc., 15 Aug. 2016. Web. 5 July 2017. <https://www.britannica.com/event/Iconoclastic-Controversy>.

Staff, Hannity. "Here's The Reason Walls Were Built Around The Vatican." *The Sean Hannity Show.* Sean Hannity, 2016. Web. 5 July 2017. <http://www.hannity.com/articles/war-on-terror-487284/heres-the-reason-walls-were-built-14400553/>.

Editors, Roman Christendom. "The Muslim Sack of Rome and St Peter's in 846 AD." *Roman Christendom.* Blogspot, 16 Sept. 2007. Web. 5 July 2017. <http://romanchristendom.blogspot.tw/2007/09/rome-was-sacked-by-muslims-in-846-ad.html>.

Editors, Revolvy. "Arab raid against Rome." *Revolvy.* Revolvy, LLC, 2 July 2017. Web. 5 July 2017. <https://www.revolvy.com/topic/Arab%20raid%20against%20Rome&item_type=topic>.

Morton, Ella. "Passetto di Borgo: The Hidden Papal Escape Route ." *Slate.* The Slate Group, LLC, 3 Feb. 2015. Web. 5 July 2017. <http://www.slate.com/blogs/atlas_obscura/2015/02/03/passetto_di_borgo_the_pope_s_secret_vatican_city_passage.html>.

Editors, Atlas Obscura. "Passetto di Borgo." *Atlas Obscura.* Atlas Obscura, Ltd., 6 May 2014. Web. 5 July 2017. <http://www.atlasobscura.com/places/passetto-di-borgo>.

Editors, Curious & Unusual. "The Passetto ." *Curious & Unusual.* Virtual Roma, 2011. Web. 5 July 2017. <http://roma.andreapollett.com/S1/roma-c7.htm>.

Editors, Vatican.Com. "The Vatican Gardens." *Vatican.Com.* Internet Dominion Company, 15 Apr. 2013. Web. 5 July 2017. <http://vatican.com/articles/info/the_vatican_gardens-a32>.

Editors, Vatican City State. "A Visit to the Vatican Gardens." *Vatican City State .* Uffici di Presidenza S.C.V., 2010. Web. 5 July 2017. <http://www.vaticanstate.va/content/vaticanstate/en/monumenti/giardini-vaticani.html>.

Editors, La Gazetta Italiana. "The Famous Vatican Gardens." *La Gazetta Italiana.* La Gazetta Italiana, Ltd., Mar. 2011. Web. 5 July 2017. <http://www.lagazzettaitaliana.com/region-of-

italy/7646-the-famous-vatican-gardens>.

Oakley, Francis. "1378 The Great Papal Schism." *Christianity Today*. Christianity Today, LLC, 2006. Web. 5 July 2017. <http://www.christianitytoday.com/history/issues/issue-28/1378-great-papal-schism.html>.

Editors, Got Questions. "What was the Avignon Papacy / Babylonian Captivity of the Church?" *Got Questions*. Got Questions Ministries, 2011. Web. 5 July 2017. <https://www.gotquestions.org/Avignon-Papacy.html>.

Alvarez, Sandra. "Boniface VIII and Philip IV: Conflict Between Church and State." *Medievalists.Net*. WordPress, 27 Dec. 2013. Web. 5 July 2017. <http://www.medievalists.net/2013/12/boniface-viii-and-philip-iv-conflict-between-church-and-state/>.

Suddath, Claire. "Boniface VIII." *Time*. Time, Inc., 14 Apr. 2010. Web. 5 July 2017. <http://content.time.com/time/specials/packages/article/0,28804,1981842_1981844_1981605,00.html>.

Ladner, Gerhart B. "Boniface VIII." *Encyclopedia Britannica*. Encyclopedia Britannica, Inc., 26 Nov. 2013. Web. 5 July 2017. <https://www.britannica.com/biography/Boniface-VIII>.

Tharoor, Ishaan. "7 wicked popes, and the terrible things they did." *The Washington Post*. The Washington Post Company, LLC, 24 Sept. 2015. Web. 5 July 2017. <https://www.washingtonpost.com/news/worldviews/wp/2015/09/24/7-wicked-popes-and-the-terrible-things-they-did/?utm_term=.d6d45c19e18e>.

Joy, Elsie. "What was the significance of the conflict between Philip IV and Boniface VIII?" *Elsie's RPC Blog*. WordPress, 28 Apr. 2015. Web. 5 July 2017. <https://elsiekeeler.wordpress.com/2015/04/28/what-was-the-significance-of-the-conflict-between-philip-iv-and-boniface-viii/>.

Waldron, Martin. "Pope Benedict XI." *New Advent*. Robert Appleton Company, 1907. Web. 5 July 2017. <http://www.newadvent.org/cathen/02429c.htm>.

Editors, Spotting History. "APOSTOLIC PALACE." *Spotting History*. Spotting History, LLC, 2015. Web. 5 July 2017. <https://www.spottinghistory.com/view/6898/apostolic-palace/>.

Editors, Vatican.Com. "The Apostolic Palace." *Vatican.Com*. Internet Dominion Company, 26 May 2013. Web. 5 July 2017. <http://vatican.com/articles/info/the_apostolic_palace-a1081>.

Boyle, Leonard Eugene, OP. "The Vatican Library." *Library of Congress*. Library of Congress, 2014. Web. 5 July 2017. <https://www.loc.gov/exhibits/vatican/intro.html>.

Editors, University of Alberta. "History of the Library." *University of Alberta*. School of Library and Information Studies - University of Alberta, 12 Feb. 2005. Web. 5 July 2017. <http://capping.slis.ualberta.ca/cap05/debbie/history.html>.

Rodriguez, Juan. "Architectural Details of the Sistine Chapel." *The Balance*. The Balance, Ltd., 11 Aug. 2016. Web. 5 July 2017. <https://www.thebalance.com/g00/how-the-sistine-chapel-was-built-844358?i10c.referrer=https%3A%2F%2Fwww.google.com.tw%2F>.

Editors, Vatican City State. "Vatican Courtyards." *Vatican City State*. Uffici di Presidenza S.C.V., 2011. Web. 5 July 2017. <http://www.vaticanstate.va/content/vaticanstate/en/monumenti/musei-vaticani/cortili-vaticani.paginate.1.html>.

Rogoway, Tyler. " The Pope Has A Small But Deadly Army Of Elite Warriors Protecting Him." *Foxtrot Alpha*. Foxtrot Alpha, Ltd., 28 Sept. 2015. Web. 5 July 2017. <http://foxtrotalpha.jalopnik.com/the-pope-has-a-small-but-deadly-army-of-elite-warriors-1733268646>.

Editors, Roman Curia. "The Uniform of the Swiss Guards:." *The Vatican*. Roman Curia, 2015. Web. 5 July 2017.
<http://www.vatican.va/roman_curia/swiss_guard/swissguard/divisa_en.htm>.

Editors, Roman Curia. "The Helvetians." *The Vatican*. Roman Curia, 2011. Web. 5 July 2017. <http://www.vatican.va/roman_curia/swiss_guard/swissguard/storia_en.htm>.

Squires, Nick. "A history of the Vatican's Swiss Guard." *The Telegraph*. Telegraph Media Group, Ltd., 7 Nov. 2011. Web. 6 July 2017.
<http://www.telegraph.co.uk/news/worldnews/europe/vaticancityandholysee/8873853/A-history-of-the-Vaticans-Swiss-Guard.html>.

Editors, Encyclopedia Britannica. "St. Peter's Basilica." *Encyclopedia Britannica*. Encyclopedia Britannica, Inc., 7 Sept. 2016. Web. 6 July 2017.
<https://www.britannica.com/topic/Saint-Peters-Basilica>.

Salinas, Taryn. "Take Amazing 360° Tour of St. Peter's in Vatican City From Your Chair." *National Geographic*. National Geographic Society, 18 July 2015. Web. 6 July 2017. <http://news.nationalgeographic.com/2015/07/150720-Vatican-360-Degree-Tour-Saint-Peters-Basilica/>.

Editors, A View on Cities. "St. Peter's Square." *A View on Cities*. A View on Cities, LLC, 2015. Web. 6 July 2017. <http://www.aviewoncities.com/rome/piazzasanpietro.htm>.

Schnürer, Gustav. "Patrimony of St. Peter." *New Advent*. Robert Appleton Company, 1912.

Web. 6 July 2017. <http://www.newadvent.org/cathen/14257a.htm>.

Editors, Weapons and Warfare. "Pope Julius II – the warrior pope." *Weapons and Warfare*. WordPress, 27 Dec. 2015. Web. 6 July 2017. <https://weaponsandwarfare.com/2015/12/27/pope-julius-ii-the-warrior-pope/>.

Editors, Medieval Times. "Protestant Reformation." *Medieval Times*. Medieval Times, Ltd., 2007. Web. 6 July 2017. <http://www.medieval-life-and-times.info/medieval-religion/protestant-reformation.htm>.

Arnold, Jack L., PhD. "THE CAUSE AND RESULTS OF THE REFORMATION." *IIIM Magazine Online*. IIIM Magazine, LLC, 14 Mar. 1999. Web. 6 July 2017. <http://old.thirdmill.org/newfiles/jac_arnold/CH.Arnold.RMT.2.html>.

Beaumont, Douglas. "The Spanish Inquisition: Debunking the Legends." *Strange Notions*. Word on Fire, 2013. Web. 6 July 2017. <http://strangenotions.com/spanish-inquisition/>.

Editors, History Channel. "Martin Luther excommunicated." *History Channel*. A&E Television Networks, LLC, 3 Jan. 2011. Web. 6 July 2017martin luther excommunicated. <http://www.history.com/this-day-in-history/martin-luther-excommunicated>.

Trueman, C. N. "The Reformation." *The History Learning Site*. The History Learning Site, Ltd., 17 Mar. 2015. Web. 6 July 2017. <http://www.historylearningsite.co.uk/tudor-england/the-reformation/>.

Editors, Encylopedia.Com. "Paul IV." *Encyclopedia.Com*. The Gale Group, Inc., 2012. Web. 6 July 2017. <http://www.encyclopedia.com/people/philosophy-and-religion/roman-catholic-popes-and-antipopes/paul-iv>.

Green, David B. "This Day in Jewish History 1555: Pope Paul IV Orders Jews to Live in a Ghetto." *Haaretz*. Haaretz Daily Newspaper, Ltd., 14 July 2013. Web. 6 July 2017. <http://www.haaretz.com/jewish/this-day-in-jewish-history/1.535641>.

Editors, Revolvy. " Reformation Papacy ." *Revolvy*. Revolvy, LLC, 2 Dec. 2016. Web. 6 July 2017. <https://www.revolvy.com/main/index.php?s=Reformation%20Papacy>.

Editors, Vatican Museum. "The history of the Vatican Museums." *Vatican Museums*. Vatican Museums, 2011. Web. 6 July 2017. <http://www.museivaticani.va/content/museivaticani/en/musei-del-papa/storia.html>.

Editors, Roman Curia. "THE BASILICA." *The Vatican*. Basilica Papale San Paolo, 2007. Web. 6 July 2017. <http://www.vatican.va/various/basiliche/san_paolo/en/basilica/storia.htm>.

Editors, Rome.Net. "Basilica of St. Paul Outside the Walls." *Rome.Net*. Rome.Net, 2010. Web. 6 July 2017. <https://www.rome.net/basilica-st-paul-outside-walls>.

Bakerjian, Martha. "Saint Paul Basilica, San Paolo Fuori le Mure, in Rome." *TripSavvy*. TripSavvy, LLC, 30 June 2017. Web. 6 July 2017. <https://www.tripsavvy.com/g00/saint-paul-basilica-in-rome-1547851?i10c.referrer=https%3A%2F%2Fwww.google.com.tw%2F>.

Editors, Roman Curia. " THE FIRE ON THE NIGHT BETWEEN THE 15TH AND 16TH OF JULY 1823." *The Vatican*. Basilica Papale San Paolo, 2007. Web. 6 July 2017. <http://www.vatican.va/various/basiliche/san_paolo/en/basilica/incendio.htm>.

Editors, Encylopedia.Com. "Gregory XVI." *Encyclopedia.Com*. The Gale Group, Inc., 11 Oct. 2002. Web. 6 July 2017. <http://www.encyclopedia.com/people/philosophy-and-religion/roman-catholic-popes-and-antipopes/gregory-xvi>.

Editors, Wikipedia. "Pope Pius IX." *Wikipedia*. MediaWiki, 25 June 2017. Web. 6 July 2017. <https://en.wikipedia.org/wiki/Pope_Pius_IX>.

Editors, Revolvy. " Prisoner in the Vatican ." *Revolvy*. Revolvy, LLC, 25 June 2017. Web. 6 July 2017. <https://www.revolvy.com/main/index.php?s=Prisoner%20in%20the%20Vatican&item_type=topic>.

Editors, David Kertzer. "Prisoner of the Vatican." *David Kertzer*. David Kertzer, 2016. Web. 6 July 2017. <http://www.davidkertzer.com/books/prisoner-vatican/reviews>.

Editors, Encyclopedia Britannica. "Lateran Treaty." *Encyclopedia Britannica*. Encyclopedia Britannica, Inc., 7 Oct. 2015. Web. 6 July 2017. <https://www.britannica.com/event/Lateran-Treaty>.

Editors, NPR. "Why Is Vatican II So Important?" *National Park Service*. National Park Service, US Department of the Interior, 10 Oct. 2012. Web. 6 July 2017. <http://www.npr.org/2012/10/10/162573716/why-is-vatican-ii-so-important>.

Brady, Tara. "Vatican forced to tighten security at the Sistine Chapel after pickpockets target huge crowds of tourists." *Daily Mail*. Associated Newspapers, Ltd., 21 May 2013. Web. 6 July 2017. <http://www.dailymail.co.uk/news/article-2328190/Vatican-forced-tighten-security-Sistine-Chapel-pickpockets-target-huge-crowds-tourists.html>.

Tierney, Brian. *The Crisis of Church and State: 1050-1300, with selected documents (Medieval Academy Reprints for Teaching, 21)* . Reprint ed. N.p.: U of Toronto Press, 1988. Print.

Gibbon, Edward. *The Decline and Fall of the Roman Empire, Volume III*. Vol. 3. N.p.: Naxos Audio on Brilliance Audio, 2016. Print.

Kreutz, Barbara. *Before the Normans: Southern Italy in the Ninth and Tenth Centuries*. N.p.: U of Pennsylvania Press, 1996. Print.

Free Books by Charles River Editors

We have brand new titles available for free most days of the week. To see which of our titles are currently free, click on this link.

Discounted Books by Charles River Editors

We have titles at a discount price of just 99 cents everyday. To see which of our titles are currently 99 cents, click on this link.

Printed in Great Britain
by Amazon